Table of Contents

Esmonde

The Origins of the Esmondes

There is a colourful story recounted in the Anna Kinsella article[1] about the Esmondes, concerning one David Esmonde who lived in the latter part of the 14th century. Apparently he was commissioned by the King to enquire into several extortions and offences committed by the Abbot of Dunbrody. The article then goes on to say, 'he was assaulted by the Abbot Cornwalshe and several of his monks, and his letters of commission torn to pieces. David was imprisoned and chained to a pillar for sixteen days. At Dunbrody there is still a circular structure, called "the prison", in which David Esmonde was probably incarcerated.' The Abbot and the monks were not called to account until 1394, when the Sheriff of the County was commanded to take all the conspirators into custody and to confiscate the revenues of the Abbey. David was also noted as being the Custodian of the Castle of Wexford.

The very distinguished family of Esmonde, a surviving branch of which still lives at Ballynastragh, near Gorey, began their connection with Wexford in the 12th century. It is believed that Geoffrey de Estmont was one of the thirty knights who accompanied Robert FitzStephen to Ireland in 1169 when the latter lead the advance force that landed at Bannow in that year. According to Philip Hore, Geoffrey de Estmont came from Huntington, in Lincolnshire, where a family of Esmondes survived and were ancestors of Lord Worhouse of Norfolk.[2]

In her article Anna Kinsella stated that 'it was not by accident that an Esmonde was among the first to come to Wexford, because Eva, the daughter of Sir John Esmonde was the wife of Robert FitzHarding, Portreeve of Bristol, who was so

---

[1] Historic Gorey 2 ed. by Ml. Fitzpatrick
[2] Hore Mss in St. Peter's College

friendly with Diarmuid McMurrough that the latter called his daughter Aoife, after Eva Esmonde.' A further erotic connection, noted in the same article categorically asserts that Eva Esmonde was in fact the daughter of Lady Godiva, a direct descendant of William the Conqueror's half sister Isabella who married William de Esmonde, Comte de Seez! Lady Godiva, who might be described as the first Women's Libber, rode naked through the streets of Coventry to highlight the oppression being forced on her husband's tenants.

Johnstown Castle

According to Donovan, the noted Irish antiquarian, the original castle of Johnstown, near Wexford, now an Agricultural Research Centre, was built by this Geoffrey de Estomont. However, Herbert Hore stated that the property was acquired from and held under the see of Ferns from the time that John Esmonde was Bishop of Ferns, in the 14th century[3] and the fortified mansion or hall of Johnstown was erected by the Esmondes in the reign of Henry VII, in the latter part of the 15th century. Anna Kinsella states that Sir Geoffrey built a motte and bailey at Lymbrick in the Barony of Forth, and his son Sir Maurice built a castle on the same site. After Maurice's death in 1225 the castle was abandoned and his son John built a castle on a new site which was called Johnstown Castle. John died in 1261.

John was succeeded by his son Sir William Esmonde who had several sons, including John who became Bishop of Ferns, Walter (of Ballynastragh) a Canon of Ferns and an Attorney for Archbishop Lecky of Dublin, and Thomas. Sir William also had a brother Henry who was Seneschal of Wexford in 1294 and Chancellor in 1310. He was also one of the deputation sent in 1317 to demand a charter for Wexford town from the Earl of Pembroke.[4]

---

[3] Hore H.F. Mss
[4] The Families of Co. Wexford – *Hilary Murphy*

Ballynastragh

This is the first reference to Ballynastragh and it may well have been Walter who was the first Esmonde to settle there. An interesting thing about Ballynastragh was that it was situated in the parish of Kilcavan (Killinerin) near modern day Gorey and in the middle ages was called Lymbrick or Lymbrick, probably a name brought to that part by the Esmondes who settled first at Lymbrick in the Barony of Forth.

Ballynastragh House. Gorey.   Co. Wexford.

Hore in his notes on the Parishes in the History of Wexford, tells a quaint tale about Lymbrick in Kilcavan.

He states that the area was formerly called Formael na bhFian, connecting it with the famous Fianna of myth and legend. 'Finn the son of Cumhal got this land before the middle of the third century from the King of Leinster, Breasal Bealach in exchange for his maternal estate of Almha (Allen, Co. Kildare). It continued as the tribe land of Finn until the close of the third century when his family became extinct.

Bishop John Esmonde

Bishop John Esmonde, the son of Sir William Esmonde was a very controversial Bishop who was appointed in 1349 and deposed in 1350. He was deposed for very little reason as was Hugo de Saltu in 1347. Hugo was deposed because the Pope, Clement VI stated that he had "reserved to himself the provision to the See of Ferns and therefore he must have it". However Bishop John Esmonde opposed the deposition and refused to surrender the See of Ferns to his successor. Skirmishes were fought and several of the Bishop's relations were impeached for their part in the disturbances. They were Thomas Esmonde Senior, Roger, Walter, Thomas Junior, Adam, William, Robert, Nicholas , Richard and Thomas the son of Richard and John the son of Walter.[5] This John was supposed to have been the man who built Ballynastragh mansion and he was married to Isabel, the daughter of Thomas Rossiter of Rathmacknee castle who was imprisoned for assisting the Bishop in his resistance to the deposition.

The Bishop eventually consented to allow his successor, Bishop Charnells to take possession of the See and was rewarded by being appointed Bishop of Emly in 1356. He died in 1362.

The Esmonde family history from 1450 to 1570 is sketchy and Hore refers to a Robert Esmonde a juror on several important cases in the early part of the 15th century.

It is asserted in the Burke Pedigree, that the modern family began with James Esmonde (lived c. 1520) who married Isabel the daughter of Thomas Rossiter of Rathmacknee Castle. Their eldest son was Laurence, who in turn married Eleanor the daughter of Walter Walsh of the Mountain.[6] Laurence was the

---

[5] Hore *History of the town and County of Wexford Vol.6*
[6] The Walshes were a famous Kilkenny family of Norman descent and their seat was

father of William Esmonde[7] of Johnstown who succeeded to the estates. William (Walter) married Margaret Furlong of Horetown.[8]

Laurence Esmonde the Protestant

They had four sons Robert, Laurence, James and Patrick and seven daughters. Patrick's daughter married Dudley Colclough of the Duffry and formerly of Tintern.[9]

During the reign of Queen Elizabeth, Laurence Esmonde, the second son of William Esmonde and his wife, Margaret, the daughter of Michael Furlong of Horetown, thought it prudent to embrace the new religion. By doing so he secured his prospects. In the words of Anna Kinsella, 'he renounced the faith of his ancestors in return for which he was appointed Major General of all the King's forces in Ireland'. His services to the crown were rewarded with a knighthood.

Robert the eldest son married and had two sons William and Richard and two daughters. Robert was still living at Johnstown in 1618. William (d.1652), Robert's son, was executor of Laurence Lord Esmonde's will when he died in 1646. William's daughter Mary married Anthony Colclough of Tintern and this connection proved invaluable to the Esmondes when the family came under pressure during the Penal times.

Laurence was very active in the Nine Years War against the Kavanaghs and O'Byrnes. He oversaw a company beaten at the battle near Enniscorthy where the Kavanagh/Byrne/O'Moore faction were victorious. In 1599 in a famous battle fought between the Deputy, Essex and the Gaelic allies, near Arklow, Captain Esmonde was shot and wounded but

---

Castlehale near Kells, Co. Kilkenny.

[7] Also known as Walter Esmonde

[8] The Furlongs were a famous Anglo-Norman family who first settled at Polehore in Co. Wexford and later at Horetown when they swapped residences with the Hores.

[9] A very prominent English family whose progenitor was granted Tintern Abbey by Henry VIII

survived to fight another day. In 1602 Captain Esmonde wrote to Lord Shrewsbury the Lord Deputy to say that he had broken the Kavanagh faction and had caused Donal Spainnigh Kavanagh etc., to submit upon their knees.

Johnstown Castle

In the same year he built a castle and a church at Luimneach near the modern village of Killinerin and near Ballynastragh, which he named Lymbrick after the original Norman motte and bailey in the Barony of Forth. In 1606 he was appointed Governor of Duncannon Fort, which was established in the late 16th century to prevent an invasion of the coast of Wexford/Waterford, by the Spanish. He remained Governor of the Fort until his death in 1646. A contemporary writer characterised him as 'an expert, prudent, and resolute Commander, of a sedate and composed spirit. . . . of sanguine Complexion, of an indifferent tall stature, compact, solid, corpulent body with robustious Limms'.[10]

---

[10] *Lost Architecture of the Wexford Plantation* by R&M Loeber in *Wexford History & Society* ed. by Nolan & Whelan

Sir Laurence, who might in modern times be described as a bigamist, married Murrought Ni Doe O' Flaherty. She was the daughter of Grace O'Malley the fabulous Granuaile and Donal O'Flaherty, called Donal an Choga (Donal of the Wars). He met Murrought during his service in the army in Connaught. They had one son Thomas who was reared by his mother in Connaught , as she feared he might be brought up as a Protestant. Sir Laurence married a second time (not having divorced Margaret) but his second wife, Elizabeth Butler the granddaughter of James the Ninth Earl of Ormonde, had no children, so in time the estates devolved upon the son Sir Thomas.

The Wexford Plantation

Sir Laurence was a major player in the plantations and acquired vast estates in Wexford, Waterford, Kilkenny and Tipperary. Sir Laurence was M.P. for Wicklow in the Irish Parliament of 1613. Together with Sir Wm.. Parsons and Sir Edward Fisher he was a Commissioner for the Plantations, one of a small group of very influential and powerful men. In 1622 he was created Baron of Lymbrick. In 1625 he built Huntington castle in Clonegal[11] which he named after the ancient seat of his ancestors in England. In this year he also purchased Ballytramont, near Castlebridge, from the Synnotts for £2,600. After his death the Huntington estate and castle was occupied as a military station by Dudley Colclough from 1649 to 1674. When the Ram family acquired their Gorey lands in 1626 Laurence Esmonde was given 13 acres in the town which almost three hundred years later became the site of the Catholic Church and schools in Gorey.

---

[11] The castle in Clonegal, Co. Carlow is currently home to the Durdin-Robertson family

Huntington Castle

Sir Laurence the Philanthropist

The Baronet seemed to have had a human side to him also. When Richard Masterson , the owner of considerable lands in the Ferns area, died in 1627, his next heir was Edward the grandson of his brother Nicholas, a boy of nine. Sir Laurence took him under his wing to protect his interests from other Mastersons, in particular Laurence Masterson. Laurence was Richard's grandson by his illegitimate son John. Richard was a friend of Esmonde and would have known him from the time of the wars with the Kavanaghs in the late 1590s. He said of Edward: 'his dead father left the trust of the child to me and I have bred him up att scoole in my house this fowre years past relygiouslye and will the next sommer send him to the college (Trinity) if it so please God.' However it appears that Edward was influenced by Esmonde's Catholic wife and he became a Catholic later in his life.

The Great Rebellion

When the war broke out in 1641, Wexford was an extremely dangerous place for Protestant landowners as the following account of the Lords Justices of Ireland attest: 'The rebells in ye county of Wexford, increasinge daily have taken the Castells of Arklow, Limbrick, the Lord Esmonde's house, and Fort Chichester, places of good strength and importance in both these counties of Wicklow and Wexford, all the castles and House of the English with all their substance are come into ye hands of ye rebells and the English themselves with their wives and children stript naked and banished thence by their fury and rage...'[12]

Lord Esmonde was in command of Duncannon fort, and loyal to England during the Great Rebellion, and his son, Sir Thomas, was a Confederate General on the opposing side. Sir Thomas had started his military career as an officer in the continental army of Charles I and for his valiant service at the siege of La Rochelle he was made a baronet of Ireland while his father still lived. He did not however come back to Ireland until 1646 after his father's death. He was a resolute Catholic and his heirs after him remained true to the faith of their original ancestors.

The fort was an English stronghold and soldiers from the fort attacked Redmond Hall, near Hook Head which was defended by the Redmonds (see that family). One of the attacking force was a Lieutenant John Esmonde, a nephew or grandnephew of Lord Esmonde. He and fourteen soldiers from the fort were hanged by the confederates for their part in the attack. Walter Roche as Provost Marshall of Wexford was responsible for the executions and it is most likely he knew Lieutenant Esmonde quite well.

Duncannon fort itself was besieged for three months by confederates in 1644 and Lord Esmonde was forced to surrender. The officer to whom he surrendered was Captain Thomas Roche. Lord Esmonde survived for two more years and

---

[12] Deirdre Kavanagh: *Monastic Dissolution in Co. Wexford* (unpublished Thesis)

was still the titular commander of the fort at the time of his death.

After Cromwell

After his death in 1646 Sir Laurence was buried in the vault of his church at Lymbrick. His son, Sir Thomas continued to fight for the Confederates and in the civil war of 1648, when the Confederates split he declared against the Papal Nuncio and was excommunicated for his troubles. In the following year he was appointed Major General of the Leinster forces to oppose Cromwell. He continued to campaign during 1650 but was eventually forced to submit. During the Cromwellian campaign the castle at Lymbrick was burnt to prevent its being used by the Cromwellian soldiers. Sir Thomas was on the list of Transplantable Catholics in 1653.

After the confiscations of the Cromwellian period parts of the estates were granted to Laurence Esmonde the only son of William Esmonde of Johnstown. He was a grandnephew of Sir Laurence.

Since the Johnstown Esmondes were Catholic most of their lands were granted to Colonel Overstreet, and later came into the possession of the Grogan family. The Ballynastragh/Lymbrick lands were also confiscated[13] and the Ballytramont property was granted to the Duke of Ablemarle (General Monck).

Interestingly it appears that Sir Laurence Esmonde had taken the lands from General Monck during the Plantation period as asserted in a petition by Monck's son in 1668 which reads as follows: 'Upon the humble petition of Christopher Duke of Ablemarle a grant of certain lands in Ireland, lately the Lord Esmond's in the Counties of Wexford and Wicklow, whereof his father the late Duke was possessed, as also arrears of pay due in consideration of the great damages he has

---

[13] The lands were confiscated because Sir Thomas was a Catholic.

sustained by one Sir Laurence Esmonde who has disinherited him in the possession of the said lands.'

It took the Esmondes 60 years and cost an enormous amount of money to get back parts of their North Wexford estates.

Huntington Castle – Seat of the Esmondes

Sir Thomas was married to Ellice the daughter of Sir John FitzGerald, and they had three sons, Laurence, James and Patrick. Laurence inherited the title and as Sir Laurence the 2nd Baronet reoccupied Huntington Castle in 1682. He was married to Lucia Butler (Ormonde). Frances Esmonde a daughter of the 2nd Baronet was married to Sir Morgan Kavanagh of Clonmullen and was mother of Charles Kavanagh of Carrigduff.[14] Laurence died in 1688 and his second son Laurence (b. 1634) went to France and entered the French Army at the age of 14. His guardian was the Countess of Devonshire. He came back to Huntington to become the 3rd Baronet.

James the eldest son of the 2nd Baronet succeeded to Ballynastragh and the youngest son Patrick, became an officer in the Austrian army and fought in the 4th Turkish War (1663-64), spending seven years as a prisoner of war in the infamous Seven Towers prison in Constantinople. He was later made a Chevalier and appointed Governor of Prague. Chevalier Esmonde had an only daughter who married General Charles Kavanagh mentioned in the footnote below.

James Esmonde was married to Barbara Vincent from Limerick and their eldest son Laurence became master of Ballynastragh in 1717. Laurence was married to Elizabeth Brownrigg daughter of Henry Brownrigg of Wingfield by whom he had a family. They were married in 1700 A.D.

[14] Charles Kavanagh had three sons – Andrew, Nicholas and Charles. Nicholas was killed in a battle near New Ross in 1642 and Andrew and Charles went abroad. Charles who rose to the rank of General in the Austrian army was the Hapsburg Governor of Prague in the mid-18th century.

Laurence was married three times in all and his other wives were Mary Masterson and a lady called Bagg. He lived to the ripe old age of 90 and was killed when he fell from his horse while out hunting.

Marcus was the second son of James and he temporarily regained possession of Johnstown (forfeited in 1654). This may have come about when the widow of Colonel Overstreet (the grantee of Johnstown) married a man called Withers, who may have let Johnstown to Marcus. Johnstown was sold to Colonel John Reynolds and his daughter Mary married John Grogan of Wexford, a yeoman and merchant, who took possession of the estates in the late 1690s.

The main line of the Esmondes had continued on through the descendants of Sir Thomas the 2nd Baronet, who in the persons of the 3rd , 4th , 5th , and 6th , baronets resided at Huntington.

The 3rd Baronet was the Rt. Hon Sir Laurence Esmonde who served for a time as an officer in the French Army. He was married to Jane Lucy Forde the daughter of Matthew Forde head of a prominent Wexford family from Ballyfad (near Gorey in Co. Wexford). He succeeded to the title c. 1688 following the death of his father. Sir Laurence and Jane Lucy had four sons – John, Laurence, Richard and Walter.

Richard, an Army officer, who lived at Ballyconlore near Gorey, was killed, accidentally it is thought, in the hall of Huntington Castle, by discharge from his own fowling piece. Though married he had no family.

Laurence the second son who became the 4th Baronet in 1720 died unmarried in 1739 and was succeeded by his older brother John who became the 5th Baronet. John was married to Helen Galwey[15] and they had three daughters. He died in 1758 and was succeeded by his brother Walter the 6th Baronet. Walter was married to Joan Butler the daughter of Lord Caher and in addition to Huntington they lived at Wilmar near Carrick-on-Suir.[16] They had three daughters Frances, Lucy and Elizabeth.

---

[15] Possibly from Carrick-on-Suir . Mr.& Mrs. Galwey lived in the Castle there.

When he died in 1767 his widow was left in 'straitened circumstances' and sold the estate of Huntington to Sir James Leslie, the Church of Ireland Bishop of Limerick.

Huntington remained in the Leslie family until 1825 when it was leased to Alexander Durdin and later bought by his descendants. It passed by marriage to the Robertsons who are still in possession of Huntington Castle today. The Castle in now synonymous with the Cult of Isis, introduced into Ireland by the late Olivia Durdin Robertson in the 1950s.

Sir James Esmonde the eldest son of Lawrence and Elizabeth Brownrigg of Ballynastragh, succeeded to the Esmonde Baronetcy as the 7th Baronet. He also died in 1767 and both he and Walter the 6th Baronet were buried on the same day.

Thomas Esmonde of Ballynastragh, the eldest son of Sir James, the 7th Baronet, then became Sir Thomas the 8th baronet. Although twice married Sir Thomas had no children and when he died in 1803 the baronetcy went to another Thomas Esmonde, the second son of John Esmonde (the eldest son of Sir James the 7th Baronet)

The Esmondes in 1798

Sir Thomas had a brother James, a priest in the Franciscan Order who was murdered by British soldiers in 1798. He was dragged from his confessional where he was hearing the confessions of men about to take part in the Rising. There is a memorial to him and to others also killed, in the Franciscan Friary in Wexford.

Another brother, John, a doctor, of Osbertstown House, Co. Kildare, was hanged on Carlisle Bridge in Dublin, for his part in the rebellion. Apparently he was in the militia at the start of the rebellion but then resigned, joined the United Irishmen and took part in the attack on Prosperous, Co. Kildare, which

---

[16] *Dorothea Herbert Retrospections*

led to a charge of treason. He was posthumously pardoned. John was married to Helen O'Callan[17] from Osbertstown, Co. Kildare. The Esmonde line descended from him as we shall see.

Ballynastragh was confiscated because of the 'rebel taint, and the sons of Dr. John Esmonde, (who had been hanged) fled to France. Sir Thomas had no family so when he died Dr. John's 2nd son Thomas succeeded as heir and 9th baronet.[18] He eventually regained possession of Ballynastragh in 1816.

Sir Thomas the 9th Baronet

Sir Thomas, the 9th baronet, married twice, firstly to Mary Payne in 1825 and secondly to Sophia Maria, the widow of Hamilton Knox Grogan of Johnstown Castle. By this last marriage he brought Johnstown Castle back into Esmonde possession for a brief period. His first wife, Mary died in 1840.

Sir Thomas gave the Catholic Church the sites and grounds for the present St. Michael's Church in Gorey, the Presbytery, the C.B.S. school and Monastery and the Loreto Convent which is adjacent to it. At the ceremony for the laying of the foundation stone of St. Michael's in 1839, Sir Thomas said: "I felt impelled to deplore the privations to which I saw my Catholic fellow countrymen subjected".

The Church was designed by the famous Architect Pugin, who visited Wexford at the invitation of Sir Thomas and Mr. John Talbot of Castle Talbot. The portion of ground so generously donated was known as 'Sparrow's Plot'. Sparrow was the person, who in Penal Times, 'discovered' the Esmondes

---

[17] Helen later married Colonel Hervé de Montmorency.

[18] Dr. John's eldest son was a Captain in the Royal Navy and was killed in action during an engagement with a Spanish frigate. One of his brothers was Bartholomew a Jesuit priest (d. 1862). His other brothers were James (a commander in the Royal Navy (d.1842))and Laurence. James's eldest son became the 10th Baronet. Colonel Laurence Esmonde who also went by the nick-name of 'Chevalier d'Esmonde' was decorated with the award of the Chevalier, Legion of Honour. He gained the rank of Colonel in the service of the Grenadiers of Guard, in the French service. The Chevalier married a French woman and had two daughters.

as Catholics and following the resultant confiscation was awarded the portion of ground which became known as 'Sparrow's Plot' which Sir Thomas bought from Lord Valentia (Annesley).

The 9th baronet himself died in 1868 aged 82 years. One of his brothers was Very Rev. Bartholomew Esmonde, a Jesuit, who was Superior of Clongowes Wood College and an eminent Theologian.

The Grattan Connection

Sir Thomas was succeeded by his nephew, Sir John Esmonde, the 10th baronet, who married Louisa the daughter of Henry Grattan M.P. and grand daughter of the great Henry Grattan, (of Grattan Parliament fame). Sir John died in 1876 aged 50.

Sir John and Louisa had four sons and three daughters Henrietta (died aged 9), Louisa who married Colonel Henry Pilkington[19] and Annetta who married Walter S. Wilkinson. [20] The four sons were Thomas Henry Grattan, Laurence Grattan, John Geoffrey Grattan and Walter George Grattan. The two younger sons both died while in their 30s. Walter George was a Captain in the South African Constabulary. Laurence Grattan became the 13th Baronet in 1936.

Sir Thomas the Home Ruler

Sir Thomas Henry Grattan Esmonde, 11th Bt. was born on 21 September 1862 at Pau, France. He married, firstly, Alice Barbara Donovan, daughter of Patrick Donovan,[21] on 21 July 1891. He married, secondly an American lady Anna Frances

---

[19] Colonel Henry Pilkington (Order of the Bath) was from Tore, Co. Westmeath where he and Louisa lived for a time before moving to London. Louisa died in 1936 aged 64. They had a family. The Colonel wrote a book *Land Settlement for Soldiers*.
[20] Walter S. Wilkinson, a Londoner was awarded a C.B.E.
[21] A J.P. from Co. Kerry

Levins, daughter of Peter Levins, on 15 September 1924. He died on 15 September 1935 at age 72.

Sir Thomas succeeded to the title of 11th Baronet Esmonde, of Ballynastragh, co. Wexford on 9 December 1876.

He held the office of Home Rule Member of Parliament (M.P.) for South Dublin County between 1885 and 1892. and Home Rule Member of Parliament (M.P.) for West Kerry between 1892 and 1900 and for Wexford up to 1918. He was Chief Whip of the Irish Party (anti-Parnellite) after the split following Parnell's death. A devout Catholic he held the office of Chamberlain to the Vatican Household in 1898 and was decorated with the award of the Grand Officer, Order of the Holy Sepulchre.

In Ireland he held the office of Deputy Lieutenant (D.L.). Following the Treaty, he was appointed a Senator of the Irish Free State in 1922. The family was devastated when the Esmonde seat, Ballynastragh House, Co. Wexford, was burned down by the Republicans in the Civil War in 1923, probably because Sir Thomas opposed the Sinn Fein candidate in the 1918 election (which he lost).

Sir Thomas and Alice had two sons Osmond Thomas (12th Baronet) and John Henry[22] and three daughters Alngelda Barbara Mary Grattan, Eithne Moira Grattan and Patricia Alison Louisa Grattan.

While Alngelda was unwed Eithne married her kinsman Sir Anthony Charles Esmonde the 15th Baronet (and their eldest son Sir John Henry became the 16th Baronet). Patricia Alison married Rear-Admiral John Baptist Heffernan. American John Baptist served as Captain of the Tennessee in the Battle of Leyte Gulf in the Pacific when the tide of war was turned against the Japanese. Patricia and John Baptist had one son Henry Grattan who became a Jesuit priest and three daughters.[23]

---

[22] He died on 31 May 1916 at age 17, killed in action in the Battle of Jutland. He gained the rank of Midshipman in the service of the Royal Navy.

[23] Patricia, Eithne and Kathleen. Eithne married a fellow U.S. citizen Michael Hartnett and they have two sons Thomas and John and four daughters Cathleen, Elizabeth, Eithne and Patricia. Kathleen married Raymond Wach and they have three

Following the death of the 11th Baronet in 1935 Osmond Thomas became the 12th Baronet but he only survived his father by one year and died unmarried in 1936 aged 40. He was a member of Dail Eireann from 1923 to 1936.

Sir Thomas Esmonde 11th Baronet

Lt.-Col. Sir Laurence Grattan Esmonde

The Baronetcy then reverted to Lt.-Col. Sir Laurence Grattan Esmonde, 13th Baronet who was born on 3 November 1863. He was the son of Sir John Esmonde, 10th Baronet. and Louisa Grattan and brother of the 11th Baronet. He married, firstly, Sarah May Spittall, daughter of Alexander John Spittall, in 1906 and he married, secondly, Pauline Netterville, daughter

---

sons Raymond, Damian and Gregory and three daughters Kathleen, Marie and Margaret. Marie was/is a Major in the U.S. Airforce.

of Joshua James Netterville and Hon. Mary Reddis Bridget Ellen Netterville in 1928 but he had no children.

He was admitted to King's Inns, Dublin where he studied law but chose the Army for a career. He fought in the Boer War between 1899 and 1902. He was Commandant of the South African Constabulary until 1914. He then re-enlisted and fought in the First World War, where he was mentioned in despatches. He was Lieutenant-Colonel of the 27th Northumberland Fusiliers (4th Battalion Tyneside Irish Brigade). He gained the rank of Lieutenant-Colonel in the service of the Waterford Royal Field Artillery. He was commander of the 10th and 11th Battalions, Royal Dublin Fusiliers which he raised.

He died on 1 February 1943 at age 79 and the Baronetcy then reverted to John Lymbrick Esmonde who was the son of John Joseph Esmonde of Drominagh, Co. Tipperary.

The Tipperary Esmondes

The story of the Tipperary Esmondes really began in Cork when Anna Maria Murphy married Commander James Esmonde the 4th son of Dr. John Esmonde who was hanged in 1798 as a rebel.

Anna Maria's father was founder of the firm of James Murphy & Company, distillers, along with two of his brothers in 1825, in Cork, where he lived and was a J.P.

Anna Maria's brother John was an interesting character to say the least. He is reputed to have been a midshipman at the battle of Trafalgar, an officer in the Royal Navy, and after some years travelling as a fur trader in the outback in Canada became Chief of a Red Indian tribe and was known as 'Great Black Eagle of the North.'

He decided to become a priest after having a vision during a severe illness. He was educated at Beda College, Rome. In due course he was ordained at Liverpool. Following the death of his uncle Bishop John Murphy he held the office of Archdeacon of Cork. During his time as a priest in Cork he spent a number of years ministering to the people of West Cork during the Famine.

Commander Esmonde and Anna Maria may have lived in Cork for a period. They had three sons the eldest of whom, John Esmonde became the 10th Baronet Esmonde of Ballynastragh, Co. Wexford. Their second son James was probably the person who bought Castle Biggs – Drominagh on the shore of Lough Derg in North Tipperary. Their third son was Lt. Col. Thomas (see below for details about him).

Here is an account of the purchase of Biggs Castle, Drominagh, from the NUI Galway study

The Smythe sale rental of July 1870 states that the original lease was from Godfrey Boate and Benjamin Friend to William Biggs dated 1711. Built by the Biggs family on the shore of Lough Derg this house was occupied by William L. Biggs in 1814 and by Dr W. Biggs in 1837. The Ordnance Survey Name Books, in 1840 refer to Castle Biggs as "a most commodious house". Edward Biggs was resident in the mid 19th century, holding the property from Sir John Power. The house was valued at £22. The sale rental of November 1853 describes this 3 storey mansion containing every necessity and a range of out offices. It was in the possession of Edward Biggs, the owner and was bought by Captain William Tuthill. William Tuthill sold the property to Frederick Smythe in 1859. It was for sale again in July 1870. At this time the Esmondes of county Wexford bought it from Frederick Smythe. In the early 1940s owned by Owen Esmonde but purchased by the Moss family in the 1940s.

The third son of Commander Esmonde was Lt.-Col. Thomas Esmonde, V.C. who was born in 1831. He married Matilda Marie O'Kelly, daughter of Peter de Pentheny O'Kelly.

Thomas fought in the Crimean War and he was decorated with the award of the Victoria Cross (V.C.) having survived the Siege of Sebastopol in 1855. He gained the rank of Lieutenant-Colonel in the service of the 18th Royal Irish Regiment.

Thomas and Matilda had one son Thomas and four daughters Eva Mary Esmonde, Matilda Mary Esmonde, Frances Josephine Esmonde and Georgina Helen Mary Esmonde. They were all born in the 1860s.

Thomas the only son was a naval officer and remained a single man until he was 48 years old. He then married Mary Alice Mansfield the daughter of George Mansfield from Morristown Lattin in Co. Kildare.[24] He died in 1918 lost at sea. They had no family.

Two of the daughters married - Eva Mary to James Comerford and Frances Josephine to Arthur Westropp. Matilda and Georgina never married. None of the four had children.

The Descendants of John Joseph Esmonde

We now revert to James who bought Biggs Castle. James and his wife Caroline Sugrue had three sons one of whom John Joseph continued the line of the Esmondes in Tipperary. The other two sons both died unmarried in their 30s at the very end of the 19th century. They were James and Charles. They had a sister Ellen Mary who also died unmarried in 1938.

John Joseph Esmonde was born in 1862. He was registered as a Licentiate, Royal College of Surgeons, Ireland (L.R.C.S.I.). He was a Member of Parliament (M.P.) for North Tipperary between 1910 and 1915. He gained the rank of

---

[24] For details about the Mansfield family see
https://www.createspace.com/4418794

Temporary Captain in 1915 in the service of the Royal Army Medical Corps.

He married, firstly, Rose Magennis, daughter of John Magennis, in 1888 and he married, secondly, Eily O'Sullivan, daughter of Dr. D. A. O'Sullivan, in 1904. He died in 1915.

John Joseph had six children by his first wife Rose Magennis and seven children by his second wife Eily O'Sullivan.

The children of the first marriage were Rose Mary, Frances, Sir John Lymbrick Esmonde 14th Bt., Lieutenant Geoffrey, Sir Anthony Charles, 15th Bt and Caroline who died in 1929 aged29.

Frances married Edward Smithers but there is no record of them having any family. Rose Mary and Caroline died unmarried.

Lt. Geoffrey was killed in action in WW1 fighting in the same battalion as his distant relative the 13th Baronet.

The seven children of the second marriage were

(1) Owen James born in 1905 who married Eira Margaret Antonia Mackenzie, daughter of George Henry Louis Mackenzie and Lilian Mary Pope in 1938. He died in 1993 at age 88. Educated at Downside School, Bath, he was Officer with the Australian Department of External Affairs. He had one son Eugene[25] and four daughters Deborah, Jillian, Vivienne and Rosemary.[26]

---

[25] Eugene was educated in his early years in Ireland (Blackrock College) and later in Australia in the Military College and Brisbane University. He joined the Australian Army and fought in the Vietnam War. He retired in 1981 with the rank of Lt. Colonel. He married Jennifer the daughter of Sir Frank Sharpe and after his retirement he became MD of the Sharpe Group. They have two sons Godfrey and Eugene and one daughter Grania.

[26] Deborah married Peter John Coutts an engineer. Jillian married Colin Rosewarne and they had two sons, Andrew and Liam and two daughters Allison and Maria. They all live in Australia. Vivienne married Charles Cresswell and they have two daughters Laragh and Dominie. They live in Wales. Rosemary married Major Robert Peterswald and they live in Australia with their two daughters Charlotte and Georgina.

(2) Rev. Donal Esmonde who was educated at Downside School. He ministered in Kenya in the 1960s.

(3) Captain John Witham Esmonde born 1907 gained the rank of Captain (Engineering) in the service of the Royal Navy. He fought in the Second World War and was awarded the Order of the British Empire (O.B.E.) in 1943 and also the Distinguished Service Cross (D.S.C.) He married Aileen Mary Harold-Barry, daughter of Harold Philip Harold-Barry and Helen Frances Mary Riddell, on 29 October 1940. As of 1976, Captain John Witham Esmonde lived at Ballyellis, Buttevant, County Cork, Ireland. He died in 1983. Captain John Witham and Aileen had two sons Peter and Kevin, neither of whom married, and one daughter Helen who was married twice. Her first husband was Paul Clark and her second husband is Lt. Col. Robert Couldry.[27]

(4) Lt. Eugene Esmonde, V.C. b. 1 Mar 1909, d. 12 Feb 1942. He gained the rank of Flight Lieutenant in the service of the Reserve of Air Force Officers and fought in the Second World War. He achieved the rank of Lieutenant-Commander in the service of the Royal Navy and was decorated with the award of the Companion, Distinguished Service Order (D.S.O.). He was awarded the Victoria Cross (V.C.) posthumously.

(5) James Bartholomew Esmonde b. 1 Mar 1909, d. 9 May 1970 unmarried. He was a Mining Engineer.

(6) Mary Carmel Esmonde b. 13 Mar 1912 married Dermot St. John Gogarty (d. 2006) the son of the very famous Oliver St. John Gogarty, doctor, writer, wit and friend of James Joyce. Dermot served in the R.A.F. and later practiced as an architect in Ireland. They had one son Michael, who lives in England.

(7) Patrick Esmonde b. 12 Dec 1914 a prominent surgeon, fought in WW2 and was awarded the Military Cross. He married Norah Cooper from Yorkshire and they have two daughters Margaret and Grania.[28]

---

[27] They have a son David and a daughter Annabel both born in the 1980s.
[28] Margaret married Col. Peter Henderson in 1966 and they have two sons Dominic

The 14ᵗʰ Baronet Soldier & Politician

The 14ᵗʰ Baronet of Ballynastragh, Sir John Lymbrick Esmonde, was the great great grandson of Dr. John. He had been brought up in his father's family home at Drominagh, Co. Tipperary. His father John Joseph Esmonde was a surgeon and an M.P. for Tipperary from 1910-1915. Sir John Lymbrick Esmonde the 14ᵗʰ Baronet was married but had no children. His wife was Eleanor Fitzharris from Monread, Co. Kildare. He gained the rank of Captain in the service of the Royal Dublin Fusiliers, Intelligence Corps and fought in the First World War between 1915 and 1918. He was a Member of Parliament (M.P.) for North Tipperary between 1915 and 1918 and later studied law at King's Inns, Dublin. He was a Member of Dáil Eireann between 1937 and 1943 and between 1948 and 1951 for County Wexford. He was Bencher of the King's Inns in 1948. He died in 1958.

Sir Anthony Esmonde 15ᵗʰ Baronet

His successor was his brother Sir Anthony Charles Esmonde the 15ᵗʰ Baronet. He married Eithne Moira Grattan Esmonde, daughter of Sir Thomas Henry Grattan Esmonde, 11th Baronet. He gained the rank of Surgeon-Lieutenant in 1921 in the service of the Royal Navy. Later he was registered as a Licentiate, Royal College of Surgeons, London (L.R.C.S.). and as a Licentiate, Royal College of Physicians, London (L.R.C.P.)

---

and Oliver. Grania married twice. Her first husband was Denis Chambers and they had a daughter Laragh b. 1971. Her second husband is Ian Greenlees and they have two sons Rupert and Thomas (d.1985 in infancy) and two daughters Camilla and Daisy.

The Queen and Princess Margaret with Sir Neville Wilkinson viewing Titania's Palace in the late 1930s at Ballynastragh.[29]

He was an elected T.D. (Member of Parliament) of Dáil Eireann in 1951 for County Wexford. In 1957 he was decorated with the award of the Knight, Sovereign Military Order of Malta.

Sir Anthony and Eithne had three sons and three daughters. The sons were John Henry, Bartholomew and Anthony James[30] and the daughters were Alice Mary, Eithne Marion and Anne Caroline.[31]

Sir John Henry Esmonde the 16th Baronet

Following Sir Anthony's death in 1981 John Henry became Sir John Henry Esmonde the 16th Baronet. He graduated from National University of Ireland, County Galway, Ireland, in <u>1950 with a Bachelor of</u> Commerce (B.Com.) degree and

[29] The author also visited Titania's Palace in Ballynastragh in the mid1940s.
[30] Both Bartholomew and Anthony James were educated at Glenstal.
[31] A graduate of NUI Galway, Alice Mary lives in Dublin and is an honorary member of the council of the ICOS. Eithne Marion is a graduate of the Royal Academy of Music.

subsequently was admitted to King's Inn, Dublin entitled to practice as a barrister. He was decorated with the award of the Territorial Decoration (T.D.) and then held the office of Circuit Court Judge for the Western Circuit. Sir John Henry was elected a T.D. or member of the Dail Eireann between 1973 and 1977, for Fine Gael.

The 16th Baronet was married to Pamela Bourke[32], the daughter of Dr. Francis Stephen Bourke a surgeon, in 1957. They had three sons and two daughters. The sons Thomas Francis, Harold William and Richard Anthony were all born in the 1960s. All three were educated at Sandford Park School and later at Trinity College Dublin. Sir Thomas Francis the 17th Baronet succeeded his father in 1987.

The two girls in the family of the 16th Baronet are Karen Maria and Lisa Marion. Both girls graduated from College with degrees in Psychology.

Sir Thomas Francis the 17th Baronet

Thomas Francis, the 17th Baronet, married Pauline Loretto Kearns, daughter of James Vincent Kearns in 1986. Thomas Francis chose a career in Medicine. He was registered as a Member, Royal College of Physicians, Ireland (M.R.C.P.I.) and as a Member, Royal College of Physicians, London (M.R.C.P.) in 1987. His career path brought him to Altnagelvin Hospital, Londonderry, County Londonderry, Ireland and then to the Royal Gwent Hospital, Gwent, Wales. He was Registrar in Neurology between 1989 and 1990 at University Hospital of Wales. His next move was to the Western General Hospital, Edinburgh where he was Clinical Resident Fellow between 1990 and 1992. In that year he moved to Royal Victoria Hospital, Belfast where he took up the post of Clinical Registrar in Neurology and Consultant in Neurology. In 1995 he graduated from Trinity College Dublin with a Doctor of Medicine (M.D.)

---

[32] Lady Pamela died on Dec. 8th, 2014 and was buried in the family plot in Gorey.

Sir Thomas Francis and Pauline have three children - Sean Vincent Grattan Esmonde b. 8 Jan 1989, Aisling Margaret Pamela b. 17 Dec 1991 and Niamh Pauline b. 2 May 1996

www.ingramcontent.com/pod-product-compliance
Lightning Source LLC
Chambersburg PA
CBHW061946280526
45787CB00004B/1744